The Usborne BIG book of Christmas things to make and do

Fiona Watt & Rebecca Gilpin

Designed and illustrated by
Katrina Fearn, Josephine Thompson, Antonia Miller,
Non Figg, Stella Baggot, Molly Sage, Amanda Barlow,
Kim Lane and Sue Stitt

Photographs by Howard Allman
Cover design by Erica Harrison

SCHOLASTIC INC.
New York Toronto London Auckland Sydney
Mexico City New Delhi Hong Kong Buenos Aires

Contents

Fairy castle Advent calendar

Make the rectangles different sizes.

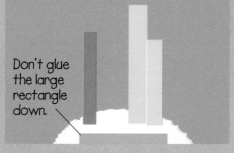

Don't glue the large rectangle down.

1. To make the snowy hill, rip some white paper to make a curve. Glue the hill onto the bottom of a large piece of blue paper.

2. For the towers, cut four rectangles from pink paper. Then, cut a large rectangle and two more towers from blue and purple paper.

3. Lay the large rectangle on the hill, to show you how wide the castle will be. Then, glue the three tallest towers onto the hill.

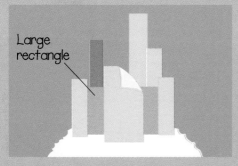

Large rectangle

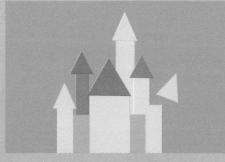

Don't make the shapes too small.

4. Glue the large rectangle over the bottoms of the three tall towers. Then, glue the three remaining towers on top of the rectangle.

5. Cut out six different-sized triangles for the roofs of the towers. Then, glue one roof onto the top of each tower.

6. Cut out twenty-four doors for the calendar. Cut out some to go in the sky, flags for the roofs and windows for the castle.

Draw a flagpole with a silver pen.

Print dots on some of the blue doors, too.

7. Spread glue along one side of each door and glue it on. Then, under each one, draw a tiny picture or glue on a shiny sticker.

8. For the trees on the hill, cut out lots of green paper triangles. Then, glue them on, with some of them overlapping.

9. For snow, fingerprint white dots in the sky around the castle. When the paint is dry, write the numbers on the doors.

Printed penguins

1. Make a pile of several kitchen paper towels on a thick layer of old newspapers.

2. Pour some black poster paint or acrylic on top. Spread the paint with the back of a spoon.

3. Cut a big potato in half. Then, carefully cut away two sides, like this, to make a handle.

4. To print a body, press the potato into the paint then press it onto a piece of thick paper.

5. When the paint has dried, use a smaller potato to print a white tummy on the penguin.

6. Dip a brush in a little orange paint and paint a pointed beak on one side of the penguin.

6

7. Use a thin brush to paint a curved black flipper on each side of the penguin's body.

8. For the penguin's feet, paint two brught orange triangles at the bottom of the body.

9. Paint a white eye. Then, add a black dot to the middle of the eye when the white paint is dry.

For a gift tag, cut around a penguin print, then tape ribbon to the back.

Make wrapping paper by printing penguins all over a large piece of paper.

For a Christmas card, glue a printed penguin onto a piece of folded cardboard.

Ice fairies

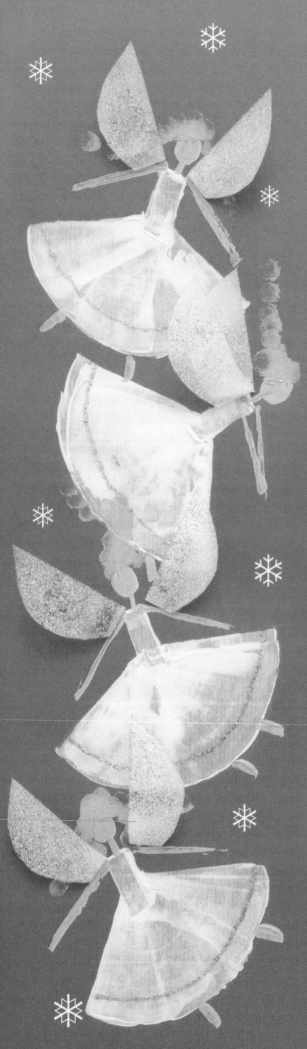

1. Pour some white paint onto an old plate. Then, cut a rectangle from thick cardboard and dip one edge into the paint.

2. To make a skirt, place the edge of the cardboard on some paper. Scrape it around, keeping the top end in the same place.

3. To make the body, dip the edge of a shorter piece of cardboard into the paint. Then, place it above the skirt and drag it across.

4. Mix some paint for the skin. Then, dip the end of another piece of cardboard into the paint. Press it onto the paper, to print arms.

5. Cut a small cardboard rectangle and print a neck and two feet. Then, dip your fingertip into the paint and print a head.

6. When the head is dry, spread a little blue paint onto the plate. Then, dip your finger into the paint and fingerprint some hair.

You could decorate the fairies'
skirts with a line of glitter glue.

The part you're holding
will stay sticky.

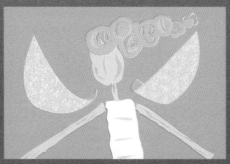

7. For the wings, sprinkle a little glitter onto some newspaper. Hold a piece of sticky tape at one end and dip it into the glitter.

8. Dip a second piece of tape into the glitter. Then, cut a corner off each piece of tape, away from the sticky end, like this.

9. Press the sticky end of the wings onto the fairy. Then, fold them back and press them down, so that the glitter is on the front.

Christmas fairy wings

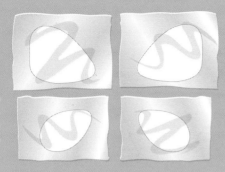

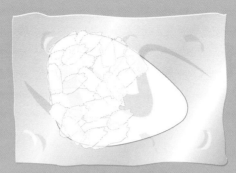

1. Draw two big wing shapes and two smaller ones on paper. Then, cut them out and lay plastic food wrap over them.

2. Rip up white tissue paper and lay the pieces overlapping on the food wrap. Cover the shapes, including their edges.

3. Mix some household glue with water so that it is runny. Then, brush the glue over the pieces of tissue paper.

Put the wings on your back and ask someone to tie the ribbons around your arms at the front.

4. Rip pieces of pink tissue paper, lay them on top, then brush them with glue. Add two more layers of white tissue paper and glue.

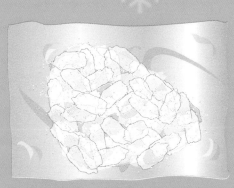

5. Sprinkle glitter over the wet glue on the wings. Let it dry, then brush another layer of glue over the top of the glitter. Leave it to dry.

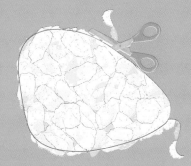

6. Peel the wings off the food wrap. Lay the paper wing shapes on top, then draw around them. Cut out the shapes you have drawn.

These wings had curves cut in the wing shapes in step 1.

7. Glue the top parts of the wings onto the bottom parts. Decorate the wings with sequins, holiday stickers or shiny paper shapes.

Use a ballpoint pen.

8. Cut a small rectangle from thick cardboard. Make four holes in it with a pen, then thread two long pieces of ribbon through the holes.

Leave long ends on the ribbons.

9. Glue the rectangle onto the back of the wings, with the ends of the ribbons sticking out. Then, let the glue dry completely.

Fairy crown

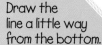

Draw the line a little way from the bottom.

1. Cut a rectangle of paper that fits around your head. This crown sits on the top of your head, so cut a little off one end.

2. Fold the rectangle in half, with the short ends together, then fold it twice more. Then, draw a line across the paper, like this.

Use hair clips to clip the crown to your hair.

Crease mark

Cut through all the layers.

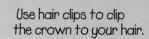

3. To mark the middle of the folded paper, fold it in half, with the long sides together. Then, press it to make a crease at the end.

4. Using a ruler, draw a line from the crease mark to each end of the line at the bottom. Then, cut along the slanting lines.

5. Unfold the paper shape, then lay it on a piece of thin cardboard. Carefully draw around the shape, and cut it out.

The cut goes halfway down.

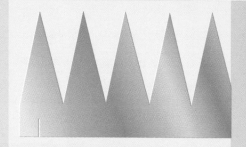

6. Cut off the triangle at one end, leaving a strip at the bottom. Then, make a cut down into the strip, like this.

7. At the other end of the crown, make a cut up into the last triangle, like this. Make the cut the same length as the first one.

8. Bend the crown around and slot the cuts into each other, with the ends inside. Then, secure the ends with a piece of tape.

Glue little beads onto
the ends of the points.

9. Bend each point out
with your fingers, like this.
Then, glue beads and
sequins onto the crown, or
decorate it with glitter glue.

13

Handprinted angel

This is the angel's dress upside-down.

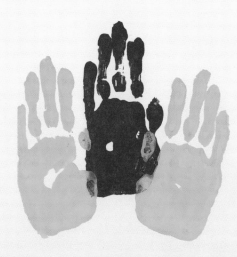

1. For the dress, press your hand in blue paint, then press it in the middle of some paper.

2. Press both hands into some yellow paint. Make two prints a little lower, for the wings.

3. Turn your paper. Dip your finger in pink paint, then go around and around, for a head.

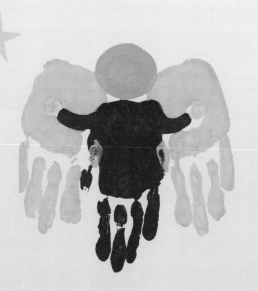

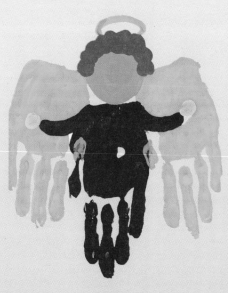

4. Use your fingertip to do blue arms. Join them to the dress. Add some hands, too.

5. Use orange paint to finger paint some hair. Then, add a yellow halo above the head.

6. Fingerprint some eyes and a nose. Then, use your little fingertip to paint a smiling mouth.

Glue your angel picture to a piece of stiff paper to make a large Christmas card.

15

Christmas tree Advent calendar

1. Cut a piece of bright cardboard or thick paper the same size as this book, when it's opened out.

2. For the tree, fold a large rectangle of green paper in half, long sides together.

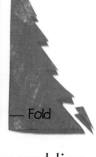

3. Draw a diagonal line, then cut along it. Cut out small triangles along the open edge.

Fold   Fold

4. Cut a white shape for the snow. Glue it on. Open out the tree and glue it in the middle.

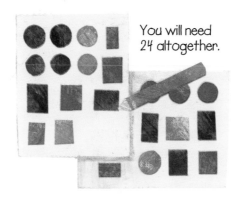

You will need 24 altogether.

5. For the "doors," draw different shapes.

Glue down here only.

6. Cut out all the shapes you have drawn. Put glue along one edge of each shape and press it on.

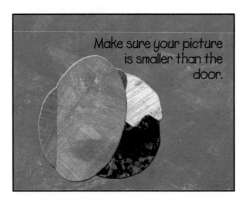

Make sure your picture is smaller than the door.

7. Draw a small Christmas picture behind each door.

8. Decorate the tree around the doors with holiday stickers and shapes cut from paper.

9. Use a felt-tip pen to write a number on each door. Start at one and go up to 24.

As you open each door during December, fold it back, so that it stays open.

Spangly star wand

1. Draw a star on a piece of cardboard and cut it out. Then, put the star onto the cardboard again and draw around it.

This wand was made using bits of blue and white tissue paper.

These wands had shiny paper glued around the straw, instead of foil.

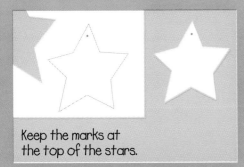

2. Draw a mark at the top of the first star, then move it off the cardboard. Draw a mark at the top of the second star, then cut it out.

The slots need to be the same length.

3. Keeping the marks at the top, cut a slot in each star, like this. Make the slots the same thickness as the cardboard.

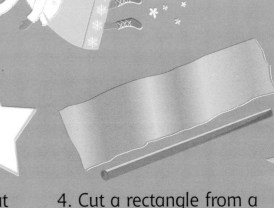

4. Cut a rectangle from a roll of aluminum foil, making it a little longer and several times wider than a drinking straw.

5. Lay the foil on some old newspaper and cover the non-shiny side with glue. Then, lay the straw on top, near one edge of the foil.

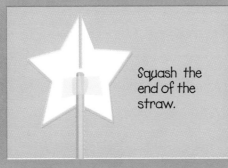

Squash the end of the straw.

6. Roll the straw, so that the foil sticks all the way around it. Then, tape the straw onto the star with a slot at the top.

Hold the straw in place.

7. Hold the star with the slot at the bottom, above the star with the slot at the top. Then, push the stars together, like this.

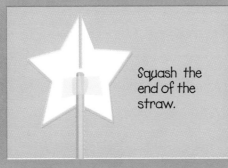

Use household glue.

8. Rip up lots of strips of tissue paper and glue them all over the stars. Cover the stars with two or three layers of tissue paper.

9. Brush the stars with glue and sprinkle them with glitter. Glue on lots of beads and sequins, or shapes cut from shiny paper.

Holly fairy collage

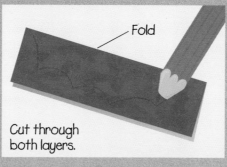

Fold

Cut through both layers.

Join the points in the middle.

1. For the fairy's skirt, rip a shape from pink paper. Don't worry if it's uneven. Glue it onto a piece of paper for the background.

2. For the wings, cut green pictures out of a magazine. Fold them in half and draw half a holly leaf on the fold. Then, cut out the leaves.

3. Unfold the leaves and flatten them. Then, glue them onto the background, just above the top of the fairy's skirt.

4. Rip a shape that is a little bigger than the skirt, from white tissue paper. Then, gather the tissue paper at the top, like this.

You could make a holly fairy and glue it to the front of a card.

5. Glue the gathered part of the white tissue paper onto the skirt. Then, cut out a body from white paper and glue it on top.

Use paper from a magazine.

Glue the feet onto some shoes.

Decorate the dress, too.

6. Cut out a head, a neck and some hair. Glue the head and neck onto the hair, then draw a face. Glue the head onto the body.

7. Cut out arms and rip sleeves from paper. Glue them all onto the fairy. Then, cut out feet and glue them on, too.

8. Cut a crown and a strip of paper for a wand and glue them onto the fairy. Add a star sequin to the end of the wand.

Printed reindeer

1. Cut a potato in half, lengthways. Then, turn it over and cut away two pieces at the sides, to make a handle.

2. Lay a few kitchen paper towels in a pile on a newspaper. Pour brown paint on top and spread it out with an old spoon.

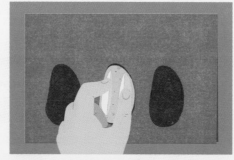

3. Holding the handle, press the flat side of the potato firmly onto the patch of brown paint, then lift it up.

4. Press the potato onto some paper to print the reindeer's head. Press the potato into the paint again and do more prints.

5. For the reindeer's ears, dip your middle finger into the brown paint. Fingerprint an ear on either side of the head.

6. When the brown paint is dry, pour red paint onto the paper towels and spread it out. Dip your first finger into the paint.

7. Fingerprint a red nose near the bottom of each head. Then, use a black felt-tip pen to draw two eyes on each one.

8. When the paint is dry, draw two long lines for antlers. Then, draw a few smaller lines on each side of the long lines.

You could print the reindeer
on a card or gift tag, or just
do them on paper for fun.

Snowflake fairies

1. Lay a mug on a piece of white paper. Draw around it, then draw around it on some purple paper, too. Then, cut out the circles.

2. To make a snowflake for the dress, fold the white circle in half, then fold it in half twice more. Then, cut a triangle out of one side.

3. Cut out lots more triangles, all around the edges of the folded piece of paper. Make the triangles different sizes.

4. Brush household glue over the snowflake. Sprinkle it with glitter, then let it dry. Then, glue it onto the purple circle.

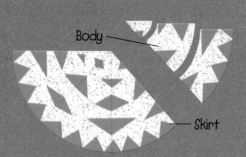

Body

Skirt

5. Cut the snowflake in half. For a skirt, cut one half into two pieces. Then, cut a shape for the body from the smaller piece.

6. Glue the skirt onto a piece of paper, then glue on the body. Cut out a purple sash and glue it on, where the pieces join.

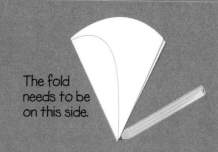

The fold needs to be on this side.

7. For the wings, draw around the mug and cut out the circle. Fold it in half three times, then draw half a wing shape, like this.

24

You could make a
Christmas card
with a snowflake
fairy on it.

Keep the
paper folded.

8. Cut along the line you
have drawn, then cut a
few triangles along the
fold, like this. Then, open
out the wings.

9. Spread glue over the
wings. Sprinkle them with
glitter, then let the glue
dry. Glue the wings next to
the body, like this.

Add glittery
shoes,
too.

10. Cut out a head and
some hair and glue them
together. Cut out arms, legs
and a crown and glue them
all on. Then, draw a face.

Glittery fairy bookmark

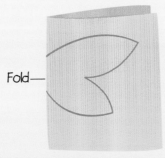

1. Cut a circle from paper for the fairy's head. Then, draw a shape for the hair on thick pink paper and cut it out.

Use household glue.

2. Cover the hair with glue and sprinkle it with glitter. While the glue dries, cut a strip from the pink paper and glue the head onto it.

3. Glue the hair onto the head and draw a face. Then, cut a crown from shiny paper and glue it onto the hair.

Fold —

Use shiny paper if you have some.

4. For wings, fold a piece of thick paper in half and draw a wing on it, like this. Then, keeping the paper folded, cut out the shape.

5. Glue the wings onto the back of the pink strip of paper. Then, decorate the bookmark with stickers, glitter glue and silver pens.

The snowflakes on the blue bookmark were drawn with a silver pen.

Pretty boxes

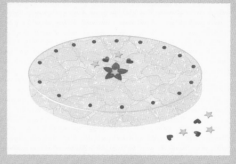

1. Rip some tissue paper into pieces. Brush the pieces with household glue and press them all over a box and its lid.

2. Brush glue all over the top and the sides of the lid. Then, sprinkle glitter all over the lid and leave it to dry.

3. When the glue is dry, glue sequins around the edge of the lid. Then, glue sequins in the middle, too. Leave the glue to dry.

You could use any small box, such as a gift box.

Fingerprint fat robins

Dip your finger in paint each time you do a print.

1. Dip the end of one finger in brown paint. Print it onto paper. Do several more prints.

2. Dip a finger into red paint and press it onto each brown shape for a tummy.

3. Wash your hands. Then, dip a finger in white paint and print a spot inside the red shape.

4. Dip the edge of a piece of thin cardboard into brown paint and print two lines for the tail.

5. When the paint is completely dry, draw the robin's beak and eyes with a felt-tip pen.

6. Draw two wings and legs. For the feet, add three small lines at the end of each leg.

You could print robins on a piece of folded thick paper to make a Christmas card.

28

Christmas decorations

Flying angels

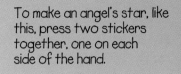
To make an angel's star, like this, press two stickers together, one on each side of the hand.

1. Draw a curved triangle on thick paper for the angel's dress and cut it out. Cut two arms from the same paper, too.

To make a wing like this angel's, glue gold paper onto the rectangle before you fold it into a zigzag.

2. Cut out hands and glue them on the arms. Glue one arm behind the dress and glue the other arm on top of the dress.

3. Cut a round head and some hair from paper. Glue the hair onto the head, then glue the head onto the dress.

Hold the layers together as you cut.

4. Fold a rectangle of paper one way, then the other, to make a zigzag for the wing. Then, cut off the end at an angle.

5. Cut a piece of thread and tie a big knot in one end. Lay the thread in the middle of the zigzag. Then, wrap tape around the end.

6. Hold the wing against the dress, like this. Get someone to help you put a piece of tape across the wing to secure it.

For a sparkly halo, bend a piece of a pipe cleaner into a circle and tape it on.

7. Draw a face on your angel. Then, cut out feet and glue them on the dress. Decorate the angel with paper and holiday stickers.

Hang your angel from a Christmas tree or as a decoration in a window.

31

Glittery star chains

Cut the paper at an angle, like this.

1. To make a star, put a mug on a piece of paper and draw around it with a pencil. Then, cut out the circle you have drawn.

2. Fold the circle in half, then fold it in half three more times. Then, cut across the folded piece of paper, to make a point.

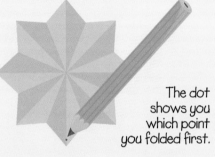

The dot shows you which point you folded first.

3. Unfold the star. Draw a pencil dot on one of the points. Then, fold the star in half from this point to the point opposite it.

4. Crease the fold, then open out the star. Fold the next point over to the point opposite it. Then, fold the others in the same way.

Press lightly, or you will squash the star.

5. To make a dip between two points, push the points together. Squash down the fold between them. Repeat this all the way around.

6. Unfold the star and gently press down on its middle, to open out the points a little. Then, make more stars for the chain.

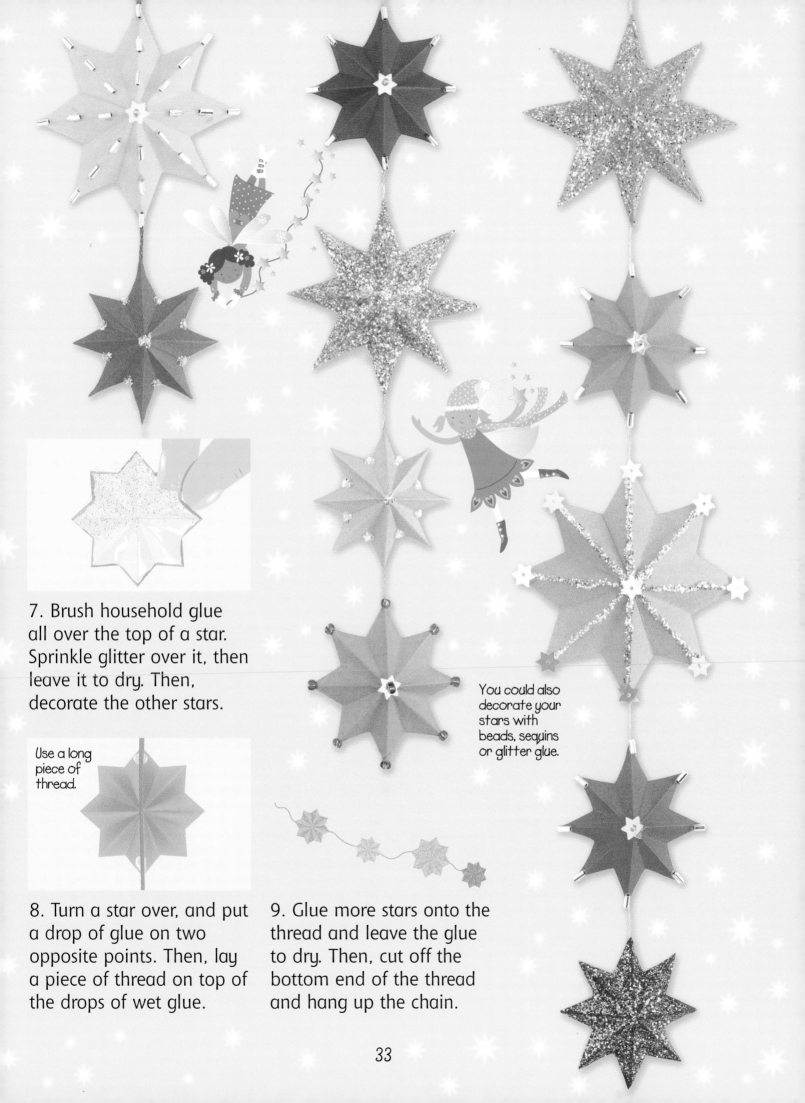

7. Brush household glue all over the top of a star. Sprinkle glitter over it, then leave it to dry. Then, decorate the other stars.

Use a long piece of thread.

8. Turn a star over, and put a drop of glue on two opposite points. Then, lay a piece of thread on top of the drops of wet glue.

9. Glue more stars onto the thread and leave the glue to dry. Then, cut off the bottom end of the thread and hang up the chain.

You could also decorate your stars with beads, sequins or glitter glue.

Fairy lantern decorations

Mix the glue and water on an old plate.

1. Mix some household glue with water, so that it is runny. Then, brush the glue all over one side of a piece of paper.

2. Sprinkle silver glitter over the wet glue, then leave the glue to dry. When it is dry, turn the paper over.

3. Mix some pink paint with a little water. Then, paint all over the piece of paper and leave the paint to dry completely.

4. When the paint is dry, draw little dots all over it with glitter glue. Then, draw a pencil line down the middle of the paper.

5. Draw three lines across the paper, to make eight rectangles the same size. Then, cut along all the lines you have drawn.

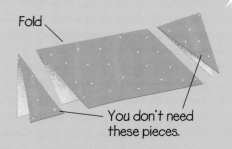

Fold

You don't need these pieces.

6. Fold one of the rectangles in half, along its length. With the fold at the top, cut a triangle off each end.

The cuts need to be at an angle.

7. Cut lots of slits along the folded edge of the paper, but don't cut as far as the unfolded side. Then, open out the paper shape.

Hold the ends together until they stick.

8. Put a drop of glue at the top and bottom of one end of the shape. Bend the shape around until the ends meet. Press them together.

Tape this end, too.

9. Tape a piece of thread inside the lantern, as a handle for hanging. Then, make more lanterns from the other rectangles.

Find out how to make this fairy tree decoration on pages 48-49.

The pink lantern below had a line of glitter glue added before it was glued together.

Tree and snowflake decorations

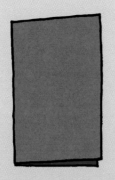

1. Fold a rectangle of green paper in half, long sides together.

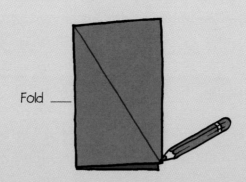

2. Draw a line from the top of the fold to the opposite corner.

3. Cut along the line to make a tall triangle. Keep the paper folded.

4. Cut a triangle in the folded edge. Then, cut one in the other side.

5. Keep on cutting out triangles along one side, then the other.

6. Carefully open out the tree shape and smooth the fold flat.

Snowflake

1. Use a pencil to draw around a mug on white paper. Cut out the circle.

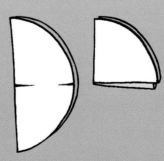

2. Fold the circle in half. Then, fold it in half again, like this.

3. Cut out small triangles from around the edges. Then, open it out.

Press small pieces of poster tack onto the tree and snowflakes. Press them onto a window.

Make lots of snowflakes and scatter them around the trees.

Glue on sequins or shiny stickers.

Christmas collage

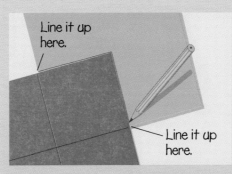

1. Draw a line down the middle of a large piece of thick red paper. Draw two lines across it so that you have six squares.

2. Put a piece of green paper under one corner. Line up the edges with the pencil lines and draw around the corner, like this.

Line it up here.

Line it up here.

3. Cut along the pencil lines to make a square. Then, draw around the square on two different shades of green paper.

4. Cut out the green squares. Glue all the squares on the red paper. Trim the edges if you need to.

5. Decorate each square with a different Christmas picture such as a star, a tree or holly. Cut them from paper or fabric.

6. To make a fan-shaped bird's tail, fold a piece of paper one way then the other to make a zigzag. Glue it at one end only.

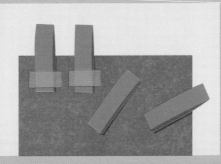

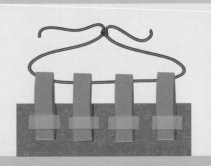

7. Add little details to each picture with glitter, glitter glue and sequins, or glue on pieces of shiny wrapping paper.

8. Turn your collage over, then cut four strips of green paper. Fold each strip in half and tape them along the top.

9. Push a long piece of thread, ribbon or string through each paper loop. Then, tie a double knot in the thread.

Use pieces of shiny wrapping paper.

If you don't have fabric, use patterned paper from old magazines.

39

Snowman paperchain

1. Lay two pieces of thin paper with their short sides touching. Join them together with tape.

2. Fold the paper in half. Then, fold each side of the papper again so that you make a zigzag shape.

3. Use a pencil to draw a snowman's hat at the top of the paper. Draw a head below the hat.

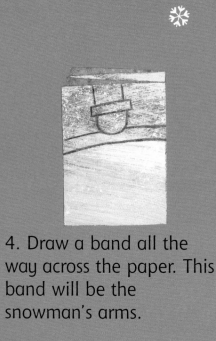

Don't cut along the folds.

4. Draw a band all the way across the paper. This band will be the snowman's arms.

5. Add a big, round tummy. Draw in some fat legs. Then, add two feet to the legs.

6. Draw around the shape with a felt-tip pen. Cut out the snowman out along the felt-tip pen lines.

7. Open out the shape. Fill in the hats and add faces. Decorate each one in a different way.

You can join your snowmen into one chain and hang them up.

Mini fairy garland

1. Using a pencil, draw a small heart and a slightly larger one on two shades of pink paper. Then, cut them out.

2. Glue the smaller heart onto the bigger one. Then, using glitter glue, draw around the edge of the smaller heart.

Make your garland from lots of different shapes using ideas from these pages.

3. Brush household glue all over a small piece of bright pink paper. Sprinkle glitter over the top and let the glue dry.

4. When the glue is completely dry, turn the piece of paper over. Draw a bell on the back, then cut it out.

Decorate the glittery side.

5. Cut a paper shape that will fit across the top of the bell and glue it on. Then, decorate the bell with dots of glitter glue.

Some of these shapes were decorated with sequins and glitter glue.

The tape stops the shapes from sliding down the ribbon.

6. Draw three stars on different shades of purple paper. Cut them out, then glue them together, with the smallest one on top.

7. To hang the shapes, cut pieces of ribbon and fold them in half. Then, tape the ribbons on, to make a loop.

8. Thread the shapes onto a long piece of ribbon and space them out. Then, tape them to the long ribbon with narrow pieces of tape.

43

Pipe cleaner trees

The star on this tree was cut out from holographic paper.

Fold the paper in half, like this.

1. Cut a piece of wrapping paper just over the height of this page and half its width. Fold it in half, with the pattern on the inside.

2. Find the middle of the fold by bending it in half, but not actually creasing it. Then, pinch the fold to mark the middle.

Keep the paper folded as you cut.

3. Draw a line from the middle mark to each corner. Then, cut along the lines to make two triangular trees.

4. Bend the end of a pipe cleaner around to make a loop. Then, cut across the top of the trees to make two small triangles.

Shiny wrapping paper with simple patterns, like these stars, works well.

You could hang these decorations on a Christmas tree or on some branches.

5. Spread glue on one of the triangles, then lay the pipe cleaner on top. Glue the other one and press it on, matching the edges.

44

Leave a
small gap.

6. Hold the trees together and cut across again to make two strips. Glue the strips on either side of the pipe cleaner.

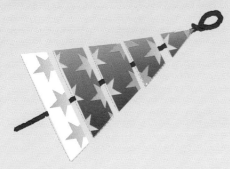

7. Continue cutting strips across the trees and gluing them on until they are almost at the bottom of the pipe cleaner.

8. Cut out a pot from some folded wrapping paper and glue the pieces on. Add star stickers on either side of the top of the tree.

Make lots of
decorations using
different shapes of
cookie cutters.

Glittering shapes

1. Press a big cookie cutter firmly into a slice of white bread.

2. Push the bread shape out of the cutter very carefully.

3. Press the end of a straw into one of the points on the star to make a hole.

4. Lift the bread shape onto a baking rack. Leave it overnight. It will get hard. Cut out more shapes.

5. Mix a little paint with household glue. Paint around the edges of the shape.

6. Paint the top of the shape. When it is dry, turn it over and paint the other side.

These bread shapes are for decoration only. Do not eat them.

Hang these on your Christmas tree or use them as hanging decorations.

7. Glue lots of glitter onto the top of the shape. Add sequins and lots of tiny beads, too.

8. Push a long piece of thread through the hole. Make a loop at the end of the thread.

9. Push the ends of the thread through the loop. Then, make a knot and pull it tight.

You could make a sparkly star for the top of your tree (see pages 60-61).

Hang the fairies on a tree with lots of other decorations.

Fairy tree decorations

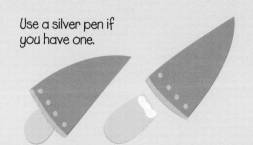

Use a silver pen if you have one.

1. Draw around a mug on some paper. Cut out the circle, then fold it in half. Then, unfold the circle and cut along the fold.

2. Draw two arms on one of the half-circles and cut them out. Decorate them with a pen. Then, cut out hands and glue them on.

3. For the body, decorate the second half-circle. Then, to make it into a cone, glue halfway along its straight edge.

Hole

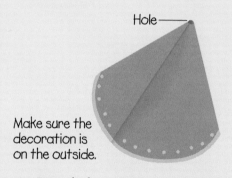

Make sure the decoration is on the outside.

Cut through both layers.

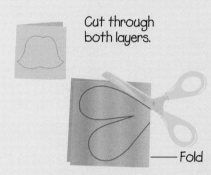

Fold

4. Bend the paper around and press the straight edges together until they stick. Then, cut off the top of the cone, to make a tiny hole.

5. Fold two pieces of paper in half. Draw hair on one and draw a wing on the other, touching the fold. Then, cut out the shapes.

6. Draw a face and cut it out. Glue it onto one of the hair shapes. Then, cut a long piece of thread and fold it in half.

If the knot slips through the hole, make a second knot.

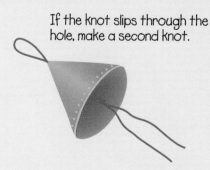

7. Halfway down the piece of thread, tie a knot, to make a loop. Then, push the loop through the hole in the top of the body.

8. Glue the arms onto the body. Glue the loop onto the back part of the hair, then glue the face on top. Glue on the wings.

9. For shoes, thread small beads onto the two pieces of thread hanging down. Then, tie knots below the beads to secure them.

Sparkly garland

1. For a round ornament, draw around a mug on a piece of bright paper. Draw a small shape at the top for hanging.

2. Cut out the ornament. Then, cut a strip of paper and glue it across the middle. Press on stickers or glue on shiny paper.

3. For the hanger, draw a rectangle with a circle on top, on shiny paper. Cut it out, then cut a zigzag along the bottom.

You could use scraps of shiny wrapping paper to decorate some of the ornaments.

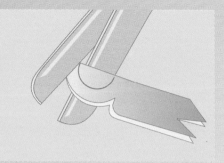

4. Fold the paper and snip a piece out of the middle of the circle to make a hole. Glue the hanger on the top of the ornament.

This tree was decorated with sequins as well as a sticker and glitter.

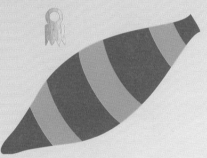

5. Draw a long, thin ornament. Cut three curved strips and glue them on. Make a hanger for the top and glue it on.

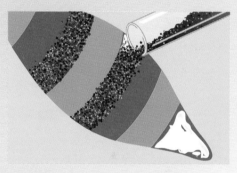

6. Spread stripes of glue across the ornament, then sprinkle it with glitter. Shake off any extra glitter when the glue is dry.

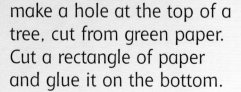

7. Use a hole punch to make a hole at the top of a tree, cut from green paper. Cut a rectangle of paper and glue it on the bottom.

8. Decorate the tree with paper shapes, holiday stickers and sequins. You could also add dots of glitter or glitter glue.

The tape stops the shapes from slipping.

9. Push a piece of ribbon, thread or string through each ornament. Secure them to the ribbon with a tiny piece of tape.

Christmas beads

Use a glue stick if you have one.

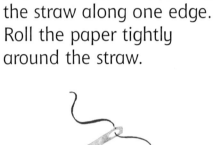

1. Cut a piece of wrapping paper as long as a fat straw. Make the paper about the same height as your little finger.

2. Cover the back of the paper with glue. Then, lay the straw along one edge. Roll the paper tightly around the straw.

3. Cover more straws with different wrapping papers. For a very long chain, you will need about five straws.

You could thread ordinary beads between your paper beads.

4. When the glue is dry, cut the straws into different sizes of beads. Cut some long beads and some short ones.

5. Carefully thread a thick blunt needle with strong thread. Then, tape the long end of the thread onto a work surface.

6. Thread on the beads until you have used them all. Put the needle through the last bead again and then tie a knot. Tie the thread onto the first bead in the same way.

52

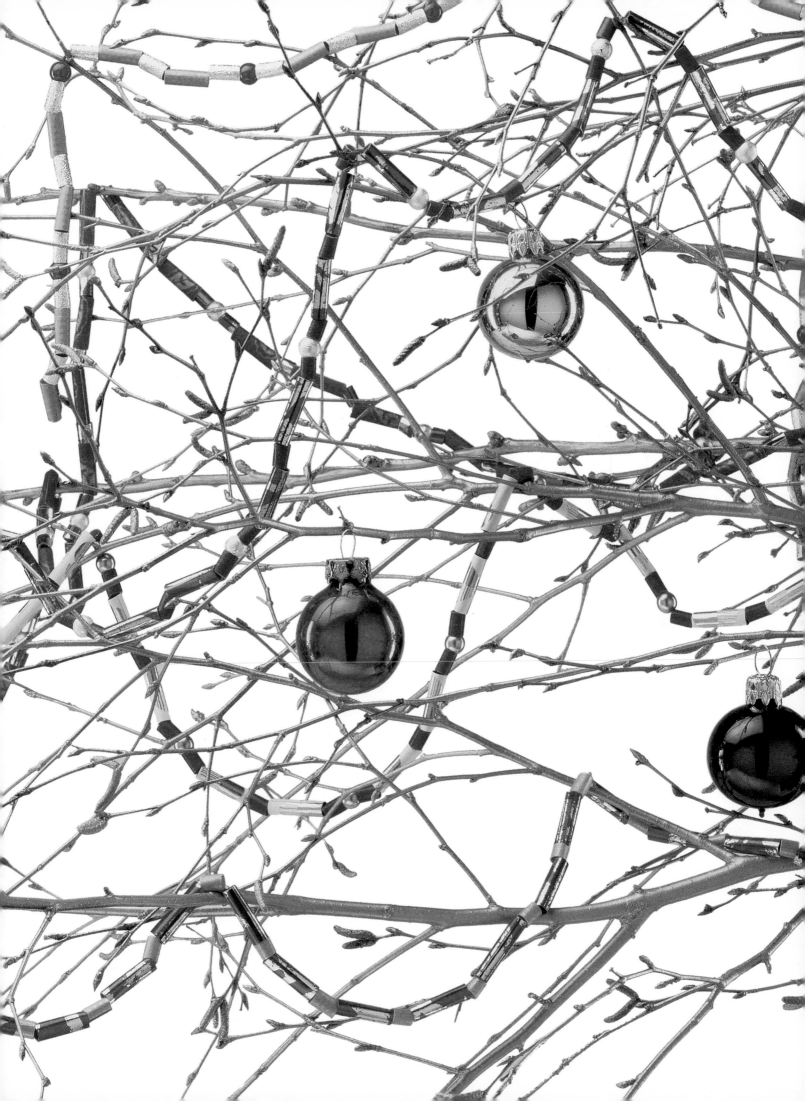

Silver trees and birds

Use a glue stick.

1. Cut a large piece of foil from a roll of aluminum foil. Spread glue all over the non-shiny side, then fold the foil in half.

2. Put the folded foil onto an old magazine. Rub the foil with your hand so that it sticks together and the surface is smooth.

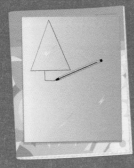

3. For a tree, draw a triangle on the foil with a ballpoint pen. Press hard as you draw. Then, draw a tree trunk at the bottom.

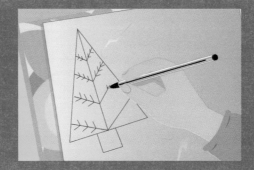

4. Draw a line down the middle of the tree, then add more lines for the branches. Draw lots of little lines on each branch.

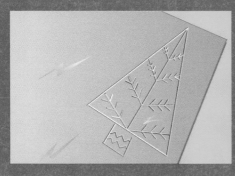

5. Turn the foil over to see the raised lines. Draw more trees, then cut them out, a little way away from their outline.

6. Cut a piece of thread and fold it in half. Tape the ends to the back to make a loop for hanging your decoration.

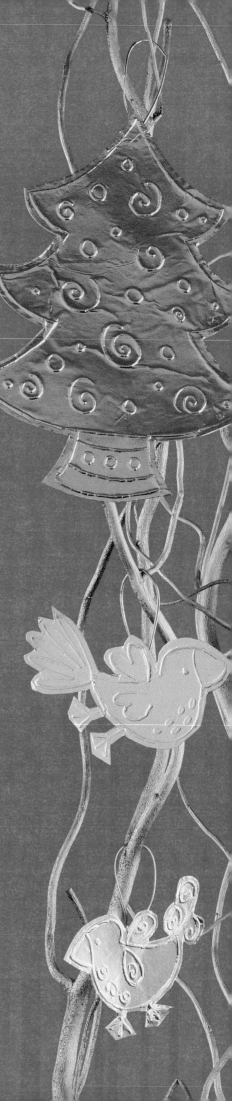

54

Birds

1. Draw the outline of a bird's body and beak on the foil. Add wings, an eye and two legs. Don't forget to press hard.

2. Add some lines for the tail, making them end with a curl. Add more curved lines on the head, wings and on the tummy.

3. Cut around the bird a little way away from the lines you have drawn. Then, tape some thread on the back for hanging.

Christmas stockings

1. Fold a piece of paper as large as this page, in half, like this.

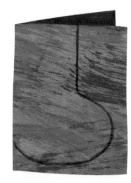

2. Use a pencil to draw a large stocking shape against the fold.

3. Cut out the stocking, but don't cut along the folded edge.

Roll little pieces of tissue paper into balls and glue them on.

Draw shapes with glue and sprinkle on lots of glitter, or use glitter glue.

Tape on a loop of thread and hang the stockings on your Christmas tree.

Don't glue along the top.

4. Open the stocking. Glue around one side, then fold the front over.

5. Rub your hand over the edge you have glued to flatten it.

6. Decorate your stocking using lots of holiday stickers, glitter and pens.

You could put a candy cane or a small chocolate bar inside each stocking.

Glittering snowflakes

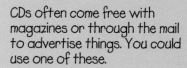

1. Lay an old CD on a piece of thin white paper and draw around it with a pencil. Cut out the circle you have drawn.

2. Fold the paper circle in half, then fold it in half again. Then, fold the shape in half again, so that it looks like this.

CDs often come free with magazines or through the mail to advertise things. You could use one of these.

3. Use scissors to cut a V shape in the tip of the folded circle. Then, cut lots of little triangles around the edges.

4. Gently unfold the paper to see your snowflake. Lay it on a flat surface and smooth it as flat as you can with your fingers.

5. Lay the CD on scrap paper and brush some runny glue around the middle of it. Sprinkle it with glitter and let it dry.

6. Shake any extra glitter off the CD. Then, put lots of little dots of glue on one side of the snowflake and press it on the CD.

7. Let the glue dry, then cut a long piece of thread and tape it to the back. You could then glue another snowflake on top.

These
decorations
were hung
from thick
shiny thread.

These decorations look
best if you hang them in a
place where there is
lots of light.

59

Sparkly hanging hearts

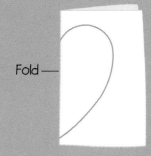

1. Fold a piece of thin cardboard in half. Draw half a heart on it, like this. Keeping the cardboard folded, cut out the shape.

2. Lay the cardboard heart on some thick paper. Draw around it four times. Then, cut out all the hearts you have drawn.

3. Fold each heart in half, from top to bottom. Then, open them out. Paint one side of one of the hearts with household glue.

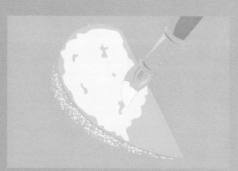

4. Sprinkle glitter over the glue and leave it to dry. Then, do the same to the remaining three hearts and let the glue dry.

5. When the glue is dry, fold the hearts so that the glitter is on the inside. Then, spread glue on one half of one of the hearts.

6. Press one half of another heart onto the glue, matching the curved edge and the fold, like this. Hold it until it sticks.

7. Spread glue on the other half of the heart and press on another heart. Then, make a loop in a piece of thread and tape it inside.

8. Spread glue on both halves of the last heart and press it on, over the thread. While the glue dries, make more heart decorations.

Make lots of different-shaped decorations (see 'Other ideas' opposite).

Other ideas

Make snowflakes, circles and stars by drawing other shapes on the folded cardboard.

This shape makes a circle with a hole in the middle.

This will be a snowflake.

This shape makes a star.

Bouncing snowman

To make your snowman bounce, pull one of its boots gently, then let go.

This snowman's scarf was made from strips of paper.

Glue buttons, cut from paper, on the snowman's body.

Make the lines about two finger widths apart.

1. For the body, draw around a large plate on a piece of thin white paper. Cut out the circle you have drawn and fold it in half.

2. Draw a line from the fold of the circle almost to the edge. Then, draw one from the edge almost to the fold, like this.

3. Then, draw another line coming from the fold almost to the edge. Make this two finger widths below the second line.

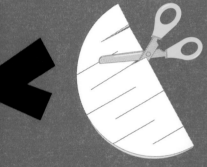

4. Continue to draw lines from the fold, then from the edge. Then, cut along the pencil lines, keeping the paper folded.

5. Unfold the circle and flatten it. Then, draw around a saucer for the head. Cut it out and glue it onto the body.

6. Cut a hat from a piece of black paper and glue it on. Draw on eyes and a mouth with felt-tip pens, and glue on a paper nose.

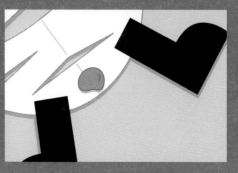

7. Cut out arms, like sticks, from black paper and glue them on the back of the body. Cut out boots and glue them on, too.

8. Cut a piece of thread or ribbon and tape it to the back of the hat. Hold the snowman's hat and gently pull the body to stretch it.

9. Before you hang your snowman press some poster tack onto the bottom of the body. This will help it bounce.

Simple snowflakes

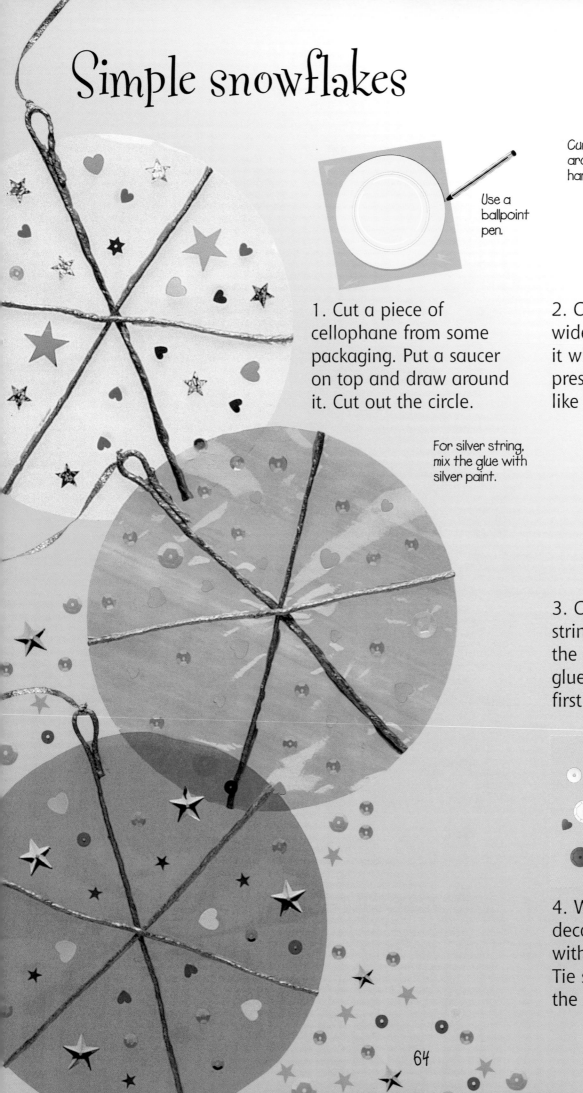

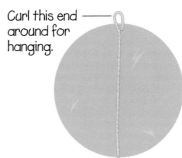

Use a ballpoint pen.

1. Cut a piece of cellophane from some packaging. Put a saucer on top and draw around it. Cut out the circle.

For silver string, mix the glue with silver paint.

Curl this end around for hanging.

2. Cut a piece of string wider than the circle. Paint it with household glue and press it on the cellophane, like this.

3. Cut two more pieces of string about the width of the circle. Paint them with glue. Lay them over the first one in an X shape.

4. When the glue is dry, decorate the snowflake with sequins or stickers. Tie some thread around the loop for hanging.

Robin decorations

1. Cut a strip of white paper about the height of this book. Bend it around to make an oval and glue it together, like this.

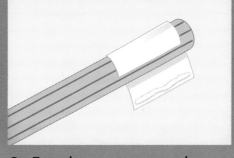

2. For the eye, cut a short strip of white paper. Roll it around a pencil and glue the end. Glue it inside the body.

You could hang these decorations in a window or on a Christmas tree.

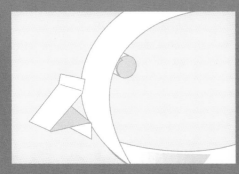

3. Cut a strip of paper for the beak. Fold it in half, then bend a little bit back at each end. Glue the ends onto the body.

4. Then, cut a strip of red paper. Bend it into a teardrop shape and glue the ends. Glue it inside for the bird's tummy.

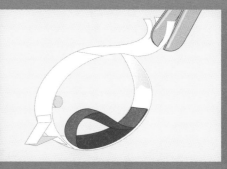

5. Glue on a strip for a tail. Make two small cuts in it, then curl the end around a pencil. Tape on some thread for hanging.

Paper angels

1. Put a small plate onto a piece of thick paper. Then, use a pencil to draw around it.

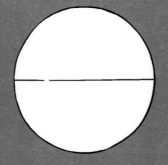

2. Cut out the circle you have drawn. Then, draw a faint line across the middle of the circle.

You could draw around a large coin.

3. For the head, draw a small circle in the middle of the big circle, just above the line, like this.

Cut along this line.

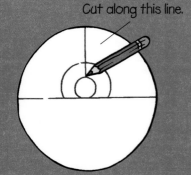

4. Draw a line around the circle. Then, draw a line from the edge to the head and cut along it.

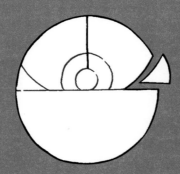

5. Draw two curved lines, one on either side of the line across the middle. Cut out the shapes.

These will be the wings.

6. Draw four triangles around the edge, like this, then cut them out. These make the wings.

Arms — Head

Don't cut this part.

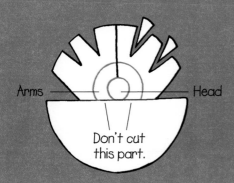

7. Cut around the arms and the head, shown here in red. Don't cut through the neck.

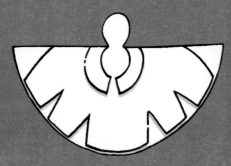

8. Erase any pencil lines you can see. Then, fold the wings and the arms forward. Crease them well.

9. Decorate the angel with felt-tip pens, or draw shapes with glue and sprinkle them with glitter.

Use thick white or cream paper to make the angels.

Use gold paper or foil to make the halos.

Decorate the angels' skirts with stars and spirals.

10. Turn the angel around and bend the ends around to make a cone. Tape the ends together.

11. To make a halo, fold a piece of paper in half. Draw the shape shown here and cut it out.

12. Open out the halo and flatten the fold. Tape the halo to the back of the angel's head.

Use glitter glue, if you have it, to add dots to the angels' skirts.

Snowflake ornaments

1. Draw around a mug twice on a piece of white paper, then draw around it twice on red paper. Cut out the circles.

2. Cut a strip of thick cardboard about the width of one of the circles. Cut two shorter, narrower strips, too.

3. Pour some red and white paint onto an old plate. Dip the edge of the longest piece of cardboard into the white paint.

4. Press the edge onto one of the red circles. Print two more lines in an X, dipping the cardboard into the paint each time.

5. Use the other pieces of cardboard to print shorter lines on the snowflake. Then, print a snowflake on the other red circle.

Use other edges of the cardboard for the red paint.

6. Print red snowflakes in the same way on the white circles, then leave them until the paint is completely dry.

7. Fold each circle in half, along one of the long printed lines. Then, spread glue on one half of one of the red circles.

68

For a sparkly
snowflake, like
the one at the top,
print the lines with glue
and sprinkle them with glitter.

8. Press one half of a white
circle onto the glue,
matching the edge and the
fold. Then, spread glue on
its other half.

9. Press on the other red
circle, matching the edge
and fold as before. Then,
make a loop in a piece of
thread and tape it inside.

10. Glue one half of one of
the red circles and press on
the remaining white circle.
Then, glue the last two
halves together.

Treetop fairy

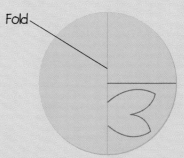

1. Lay a plate on some paper and draw around it. Cut out the circle. Then, fold the circle in half and open it out.

Find out how to make these tree decorations on pages 60-61 and page 72.

2. Using a pencil, draw a line from the middle of the circle to its edge. Then, draw a wing below the line, touching the fold.

Fold

Cut here.

3. Cut up along the fold, around the wing, along the fold again and along the line. Then, cut halfway down the wing, like this.

Line up this edge and the fold.

4. Bend the wing over and gently hold it down, like this. Then, carefully draw around the edge of the wing with a pencil.

— Cut here.

5. Open out the paper shape and cut around the second wing. Then, cut halfway down into the wing, like this.

6. Bend the body around so that the cuts in the wings are touching. Slot them together, then curve the body with your hands.

Draw a face.

7. Cut out a head and hair, and glue them together. Cut out arms and glue hands onto them, then glue everything onto the body.

8. Cut out legs and shoes. Draw stripes on the legs, then glue the legs onto the shoes. Then, tape the legs inside the body.

For glittery legs, like these, spread glue on the legs then sprinkle them with glitter.

9. Cut out a crown and a wand from shiny paper and glue them on. Then, decorate the fairy with holiday stickers and sequins.

71

Sparkly decorations

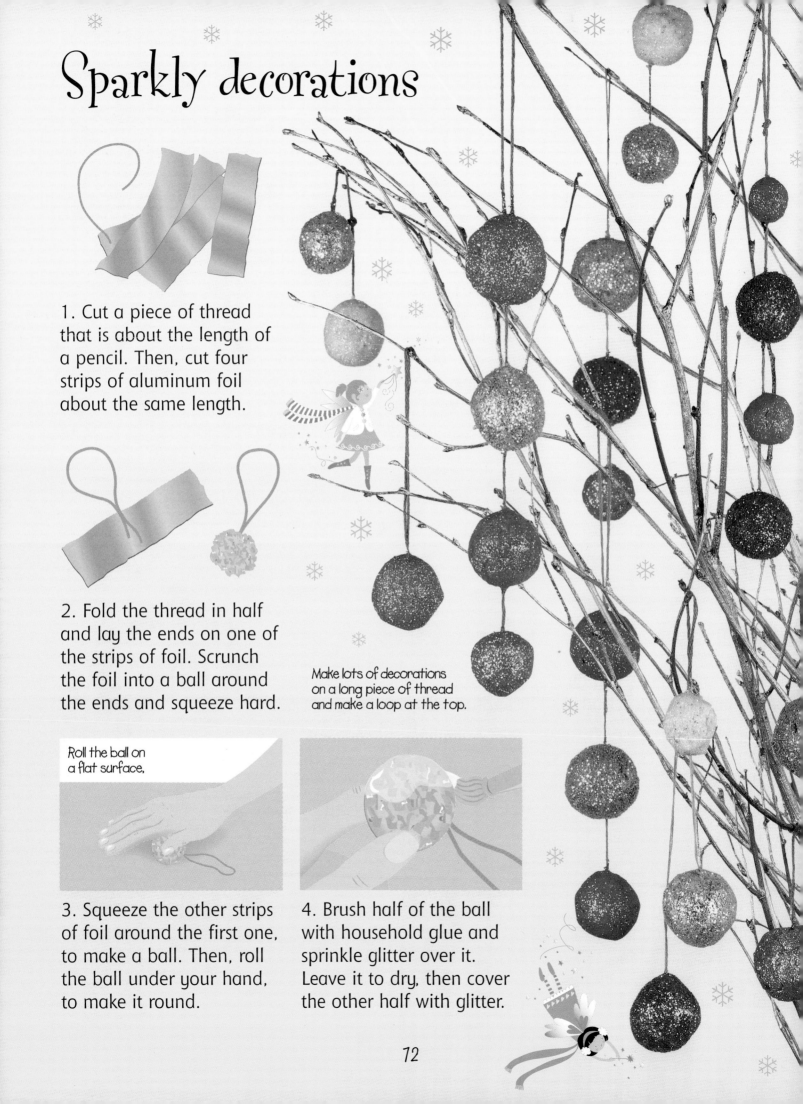

1. Cut a piece of thread that is about the length of a pencil. Then, cut four strips of aluminum foil about the same length.

2. Fold the thread in half and lay the ends on one of the strips of foil. Scrunch the foil into a ball around the ends and squeeze hard.

Make lots of decorations on a long piece of thread and make a loop at the top.

Roll the ball on a flat surface,

3. Squeeze the other strips of foil around the first one, to make a ball. Then, roll the ball under your hand, to make it round.

4. Brush half of the ball with household glue and sprinkle glitter over it. Leave it to dry, then cover the other half with glitter.

72

Christmas cards and wrapping paper

Shiny ornament card

1. For a long card, fold a rectangle of thick paper in half, with its long sides together, and crease the fold well.

The strings on these cards were drawn with gold and silver pens.

74

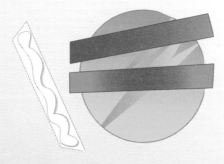

2. Draw around several small jar lids on the back of pieces of wrapping paper. Cut out the circles you have drawn.

3. For a striped ornament, cut strips of shiny paper. Glue them across one of the circles, letting the strips overlap the edges.

4. When the glue is dry, turn the ornament over. Then, cut off the ends of the strips which overlap the edge of the circle.

5. To make an ornament with stars, press stickers onto one of your shiny circles. Make some of them overlap the edges.

6. Trim off all the extra pieces of the stickers which are overlapping the edges of the circle, as you did before.

7. Decorate the other shiny circles with different patterns of stripes, stars and circles. Use stickers or cut shapes from paper.

8. Glue the circles onto the card at different levels. Use a felt-tip pen to draw a string from the top of the card to each ornament.

Polar bear pop-up card

The pieces of paper should be the same size.

1. Fold a piece of white or cream paper in half. Do the same with a piece of blue paper.

2. On the white or cream paper, draw half of a bear's head against the fold, like this.

Keep the paper folded as you cut.

Nose cut

3. Cut around the head. Make a cut for a nose. Cut out shapes along the edge for fur, too.

The polar bear pops up in the middle of the card. You'll need to decorate the front, too.

Follow the steps on page 88 for a glitter star.

4. Lift the nose and fold it flat onto the front, like this. Crease the fold. Fold it behind, too.

5. Open out the head. Push a finger through the nose from the back, so that it stands up.

Press on a holiday sticker.

Glue on a paper shape (see page 36). Dab on thick white paint for snow. Sprinkle it with sugar.

6. Use felt-tip pens to draw a mouth and eyes. Carefully fill in the nose.

7. Put glue on the back of the head, but not on the nose. Press the head onto the blue paper.

8. Cut a rectangle of wrapping paper for a present. Glue it on below the head.

9. Cut two paws from white paper. Glue them on. Add claws with a black felt-tip pen.

Sparkling card

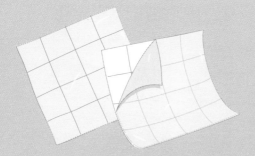

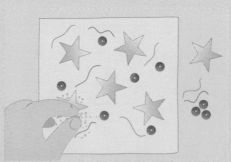

1. Cut two squares of clear book covering film. Make them the same size. Then, peel the backing paper off one of them.

2. Lay the film on a table, sticky-side up. Press lots of sequins and little pieces of thread onto the film. Then, sprinkle on some glitter.

3. Peel the backing paper off the other piece of film and lay it, sticky-side down, on the decorated piece of film.

These cards really sparkle if you sprinkle lots of glitter over the film.

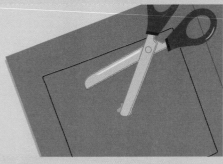

4. Fold a piece of thick paper in half. Open it out again and draw around the film, on the left-hand side, like this.

5. Push a sharp pencil into the middle of the shape to make a hole. Then, push the blade of some scissors into the hole.

6. Cut a "window" in the paper, smaller than the shape you drew. Don't worry if the sides don't make a perfect square.

Here are some ideas of different shapes of windows cut into some cards.

7. Glue around the window, then press on the decorated film. Then, cut a square of paper and glue it over the film.

You could use this technique to make gift tags, too.

Santa card

1. Fold a square of thick paper in half to make a card. Cut a curved hat from red paper and glue it near the top.

2. Cut a beard with a wavy outline from white paper. Glue it on the card below the hat, leaving a gap between the two.

3. Cut a wavy strip from white paper and glue it on the hat. Cut out and glue a white circle to the hat.

4. Cut out a nose from red paper and glue it on. Cut out and glue on two colored circles for eyes. Then, add a smile with a red felt-tip pen.

Try cutting out different shapes of Santa hats.

Tree card

Save this half for later.

Spread the paint with the back of a spoon.

1. Cut a big rectangle of thick paper or thin cardboard. Fold it in half, long sides together.

2. Get some help to cut a large potato in half from end to end. Cut one half into a tall triangle.

3. Lay some kitchen paper towels onto some old newspapers. Pour green paint on top.

Dip the potato into the paint each time you print a shape.

4. Dip the potato into the paint and press it onto your card. Print more trees along the card.

Add a holiday sticker to the top of a tree.

Print a row of trees on bright paper.

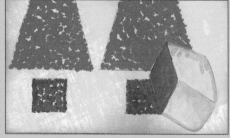

5. Cut a square of potato. Dip it in red paint and print it below each tree.

Painted snow fairy card

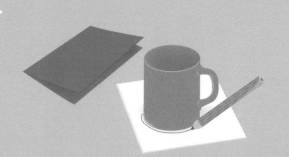

1. For the card, fold a piece of blue paper in half. Then, lay a mug on a piece of white paper. Draw around it, then cut out the circle.

2. Mix some paint for the fairy's face and body. Paint a face on the circle. Then, paint a body below it, like this.

3. Paint four shapes for the fairy's wings. Then, paint the hair and a small yellow circle for the end of the wand.

You could paint little white dots around the circle, instead of printing snowflakes.

Try painting fairies with their wands and arms in different positions.

4. When the paint is dry, outline the fairy's body, chin and wings with a black felt-tip pen. Decorate her dress, too.

5. Draw a face, then add arms, legs and lines on the fairy's hair. Then, draw a wand with a star on the end, like this.

6. Glue the circle onto the folded card. Then, paint a thin white line down from the top of the card and add a bow.

7. To print the snowflakes, cut a small piece of thick cardboard. Dip the end of it into some white paint, then press it onto the card.

You could print a mixture of snowflakes and dots on the card.

8. Print a second line across the first one and add a third line. Print lots more snowflakes around the circle.

Zigzag card

To make the card stand up, pull the front layer forward to make a zigzag.

1. Cut a long, thin rectangle of thick paper or very thin cardboard. Fold it in half lengthways and crease the fold well.

Middle fold

2. Fold the top layer over until it meets the middle fold. Turn the card over and fold it in the same way, to make a zigzag.

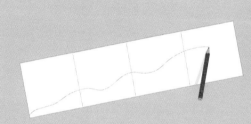

3. Open the card and draw a wavy line from one side of the card to the other, like this. Use a pencil and press lightly.

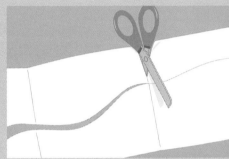

4. Cut along the line you have drawn but stop at the last fold. Then, cut down the fold from the top, as far as the pencil line.

The shapes are shown in yellow here so you can see them.

5. Fold the card into a zigzag again. Then, use a white wax crayon to draw some stars and a moon. Press hard as you draw.

6. Open the card, then paint over the stars and moon with blue paint as far as the pencil line. The shapes will resist the paint.

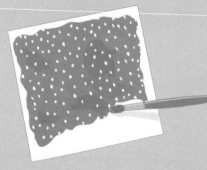

7. While the sky is drying, draw lots of dots on some thick paper with the white wax crayon. Then, paint green paint over the top.

If you want to draw lines on the trees, like those on two of these cards, cut out the triangles before you draw them at step 7.

Overlap the little trees.

8. When the paint is dry, cut out about eight little triangles for the trees. Make them slightly different sizes.

9. Glue three of the trees onto the back layer of the card. Then, glue another one on the layer in front, like this.

10. Lay the rest of the trees on the top two layers so that they don't overlap any of the other trees. Then, glue them on.

Reindeer wrapping paper

1. Use a crayon to draw the body. Add a neck.

2. Draw the head and add two ears.

3. Add four long legs and a tail.

4. Crayon hooves, a nose and two eyes.

5. Draw jagged antlers on its head.

6. Add spikes to the antlers. Fill in with pens.

Make a long thin card.

Make a gift tag to match the paper.

To draw a fir tree

1. Draw the trunk of a tree with a crayon.

2. Add branches with a wax crayon.

3. Draw dark green branches over the top.

Draw lots of reindeer and trees on small pieces of paper. Then, glue them onto a large piece of bright wrapping paper.

Tie some ribbon around your present.

Gift tags

Stars

You could write a name in the middle of the star.

1. Press the sharp edge of a star-shaped cookie cutter into half a potato. Press it in well.

2. Spread thick paint on an old plate. Press the star into the paint then press it onto thin cardboard.

3. Before the paint dries, sprinkle it with lots of glitter. Then, shake off any extra glitter.

4. When it's dry, cut around the star, a little way away from the glitter. Tape a ribbon on the back.

Snowmen

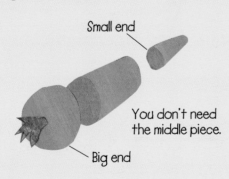

Small end

You don't need the middle piece.

Big end

1. Cut the ends off a big, thick carrot, so that you have a big end and a small one.

2. Dip the big end of the carrot into thick paint. Then, press it onto thin cardboard, for a body.

Use pens to draw the face, hat and buttons.

3. Print a head with the small end. When it's dry, draw on eyes, a nose, mouth, a hat and buttons.

Round tags

Put the paint on an old plate.

1. Dip the edge of a piece of thick cardboard into gold paint. Print a crisscross pattern on thin cardboard.

2. When the paint is dry, put a small lid onto the piece of cardboard and draw around it. Cut out the circle.

3. Use felt-tip pens to decorate the circle. Draw stripes and zigzags. Tape ribbon on the back.

Try drawing different faces on the snowman tags.

89

Printed star wrapping paper

Make the slice as thick as your thumb.

1. You will need a large cookie cutter and a potato, which is bigger than the cutter.

2. Carefully cut a slice from the middle of the potato. Press the cookie cutter into the slice.

3. Push out the shape you have cut. You may need some help with the last two steps.

Try printing with gold or silver poster paint.

4. Dab both sides of the potato shape on some kitchen paper towels to dry it.

5. Press a fork into the shape. This will stop you from getting too messy when you print.

6. Pour two or three small patches of paint onto an old newspaper. Do them close together.

You could wrap your presents in your printed paper and tie a shiny ribbon around them.

7. Dip the potato shape into the middle of the paint, then press it onto a piece of paper.

8. Dip the shape into the paint again, then print it. Fill the paper with lots of printed shapes.

The papers below were printed with a potato cut with a Christmas tree cookie cutter.

Snowman card

Press star stickers in the sky around the snowman.

You could add stick arms with a felt-tip pen.

Cut a hat from black paper and glue it on.

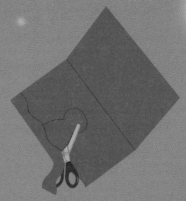

1. Cut a rectangle from blue paper. Then, cut a piece of thick white paper exactly the same size. Fold both of them in half.

2. Open the blue paper. Draw a wavy line across one side of the card for snow. Draw the outline of a snowman on the line.

3. Use scissors to cut along the line for the snow, then around the snowman and along the line for snow again.

4. Spread glue over the bottom half of the blue card. Then, press one side of the white card onto it, matching the edges.

5. Spread glue over the top of the blue card, around the snowman. Then, close the card, pressing it down onto the white card.

This card had two snowman shapes drawn on the wavy line (see step 2).

6. Draw eyes and a line of dots for the mouth. Add a nose and a hat and buttons.

Spots and stars card

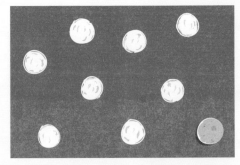

1. Cut two small potatoes in half. Then, use an old spoon to spread a patch of white paint onto a pile of kitchen paper towels.

2. Dip the cut side of one of the potatoes into the paint. Press it onto a large piece of red paper, then lift it off.

3. Dip the potato into the paint again and do another print. Do this lots of times until the paper is covered in white spots.

Use a different potato for each paint.

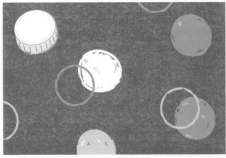

4. Spread some silver and blue paint onto the paper towels and print lots more spots. Make some of them overlap the white ones.

5. For the circles, dip the edge of a bottle top into one of the paints and print it, overlapping some of the spots.

6. For the stars, dip the edge of a piece of cardboard into some paint and print a line. Print two more lines in an X on top.

You could cut out a circle as a gift tag and attach it to a present with a ribbon.

7. Leave the paint to dry, then cut the paper into several rectangles. Fold each rectangle in half to make a card.

Instead of making cards, you could use the whole sheet of paper as wrapping paper.

Wrapping ideas

Spotted paper and tag

1. Wrap your present. Then, rip lots of circles from a different piece of wrapping paper.

2. Glue the circles all over the wrapped present. Make the circles bend over the edges of the present.

3. Rip lots of smaller circles from a different color of paper. Then, glue them onto the bigger circles.

Springy gift tags

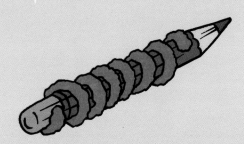

1. Cut a star from thin cardboard. Decorate it with felt-tip pens, stickers or glitter.

2. Wind a pipe cleaner tightly around a pencil or felt-tip pen. Then, slide it off gently.

3. Push the last two coils of the pipe cleaner together at one end. Glue it to the back of the star.

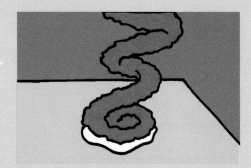

4. Do the same to the coils at the other end. Put some glue on it and press it on your present.

Make a springy gift tag which matches your wrapping paper.

Tissue paper present

Press shiny star stickers onto each circle.

1. Cut a large square from a double layer of tissue paper. Lay your present in the middle.

2. Gather the paper up around the present, then tie it tightly with a piece of gift ribbon.

Use tissue paper to wrap oddly shaped presents, such as a mug.

For a different springy tag, cut out a Christmas tree and decorate it with felt-tip pens or stickers.

Star card

Shake off the extra glitter when the glue is dry.

1. Draw three stars on a piece of bright paper and cut them out.

2. Put a blob of glue on each star and sprinkle it with glitter.

3. Cut three strips of thin paper. Glue a strip to the back of each star.

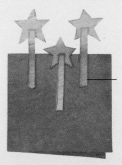

Glue under here.

Cut out a tree shape. Make lots of stars and glue them on.

4. Fold a piece of thick paper in half. Glue the stars onto it, like this.

5. When the glue is dry, stand the card up. The stars fall forward.

Tape a star onto a present. Write a name on it.

Index

ISBN 0-439-81506-1

12 11 10 9 8 7 6 5 4 3 2 1   5 6 7 8 9 10/0

Printed in the U.S.A.   08

First Scholastic printing, December 2005